meditation
TO GO

meditation
TO GO

Christina Rodenbeck

An Hachette Livre UK Company

First published in Great Britain in 2008 by
Gaia Books, a division of Octopus Publishing Group Ltd
2–4 Heron Quays, London E14 4JP
www.octopusbooks.co.uk

Distributed in the United States and Canada by
Sterling Publishing Co., Inc.
387 Park Avenue South, New York, NY 10016-8810

This material was previously published as *A Gaia Busy Person's Guide: Meditation*

ISBN: 978-185675-296-1

A CIP catalogue record for this book is available from the British Library

Printed and bound in China

10 9 8 7 6 5 4 3 2 1

Cautionary note:
All reasonable care has been taken in the preparation of this book, but the information it contains is not meant to take the place of medical care under the direct supervision of a doctor. Before making any changes in your health regime, always consult a doctor. While all the therapies detailed in this book are completely safe if done correctly, you must seek professional advice if you are in any doubt about any medical condition. Any application of the ideas and information contained in this book is at the reader's sole discretion and risk.

Direction Patrick Nugent, Jo Godfrey Wood
Production Aileen O'Reilly
Editors Jo Godfrey Wood, Camilla Davis
Design Phil Gamble
Photography Ruth Jenkinson

Contents

Introduction

Meditation has been described as 'no-mind' or 'not-thinking'. It is a stilling of the mind for a sustained period. In essence this is achieved, at least initially, by concentrating on one thing – a word, a symbol, an action such as breathing – so that everything else falls away. This is called the 'one-pointed mind' and it is, in fact, quite difficult to accomplish.

That is why, over millennia, practitioners have developed tried and tested techniques to create this state.

Mastering meditation can sometimes feel like coming home. You feel as if you have simply rediscovered something that has always been there. The door into the tranquillity that you know is already within you has been opened.

This feeling of recall or 'coming home' is because, undoubtedly, you have entered the meditative part of your mind on numerous occasions. For example, skiing down a tricky slope, climbing a rockface, even a hard game of squash, can bring on a meditative state. Repetitive yet absorbing tasks such as knitting, chopping wood or kneading bread also have the effect of relaxing the body and focusing the

mind. People who work with their hands, such as craftsmen or labourers, are often, unknowingly, good at meditation.

You may even experience meditation on your commute to work as you sit still in the hectic peak of rush hour, or

perhaps when you cook dinner as you concentrate on getting the right consistency for a sauce. You may have lost yourself in a sunset or a gorgeous work of art, simply absorbing the colours. Playing or listening to music can also induce a meditative state.

In particular, any creative activity, if you have completely surrendered to the flow of it, can be very meditative. For example, if you are a painter, a musician or a composer you will know that in the midst of creation, you are not thinking, but the work is simply flowing through you. Allowing this to happen can be quite a challenge, which is why meditating before sitting down to do such work can be very helpful.

However, resting the mind for 20 minutes or more at a time is actually difficult. Your mind does not like to be switched off; it will constantly interrupt your meditation, demanding your attention. Most of the time we just can't sustain the required sense of being here, now. That is where formal meditation comes in.

YOUR BUSY LIFESTYLE

The aim of this book is to help you integrate meditation into your own busy lifestyle. You should have to change as little as possible in order to start using the methods described. As you grow in confidence, and discover the real benefits of meditation, you will probably decide to devote more time to it and perhaps decide to delve deeper

meditate, but most will have trouble learning to switch off the mind. Don't be put off; everyone can meditate and you are certain to benefit.

Once you feel confident about basic sitting meditation you should use it as a touchstone. You'll know how relaxed and mentally alert you can be, so you will be able to recall that state instantly. It's like learning to ride a bicycle – once you know it should feel like sailing along on two wheels, you recognise the feeling instantly.

There are as many ways to meditate as there are to make an omelette, but some are more appropriate for particular situations than others. This book offers you a variety of techniques, based mainly on Hindu, Buddhist or Taoist sources, but it is not its purpose to explore the spiritual side of meditation. In fact, there does not need to be any religious dimension to the practice at all. However, if you choose to include it as part of your spiritual practice, it can greatly enrich your sense of awareness and joy.

You may find certain methods more, or less, effective – this is largely down to a matter of character and tempera- ment. For example, visualisations

into its philosophical roots.

To begin with, it is best if you decide to put aside a certain amount of time every day for a fortnight, in order to practise the basic meditation outlined in Chapter One. Some people will find it surprisingly easy to sit down and

involve using your visual imagination
while in a calm meditative state and are
very effective, but only for some people.
Yoga breathing techniques, on the other
hand, seem to work across the board.

All the techniques in this book are
practical and will deliver results if they
suit you. The best thing to do is try

them out. So read through the whole
book: you may find inspiration on an
unlikely page. Over time you will be
able to refine your repertoire of
meditations, so that you can choose
ones that are appropriate for each time,
place and circumstance.

CHAPTER ONE

Introducing Meditation

It sounds ridiculously simple: you sit down, focus your mind on one thing for a while and, hey presto! You feel much better. But anyone who has tried meditating knows that somehow it's just not that easy. That's why it is useful to master certain techniques that have been tried and tested over the centuries.

Somewhere within each of our minds there is a sanctuary away from the noise and disruption of our own busy thought processes. Meditation is about calming the chatter of your mind and rediscovering that calm, still space. You have the ability to create that tranquillity for yourself, during your busy day.

In itself, this knowledge can make you feel more powerful. Remember that this space is there all the time. When you meditate, you are simply opening the door, walking in and settling down for a while in your own inner sanctuary. One well known technique for calming the mind is to imagine doing this quite literally.

However, you may need to be given the key to that door. There are many keys that work, most based on methods perfected in Asia over the course of many centuries, if not millennia. But since the 1960s, meditation has become widely practised in the West and people have adapted ancient techniques to suit modern lifestyles.

It is up to you to try out different keys and see which ones work for you. You may well find that in different situations you respond more quickly to different techniques, so it may take a little trial and error to discover what works best.

The benefits of meditation

Once you have found your own inner stillness, you will be able to access it again and again and with ever greater ease. This brings with it many far-reaching and profound benefits. You will start to notice some changes within yourself fairly quickly; others will take more time. If you are so inclined, it is worth keeping a diary, so that after some experience of meditating you can look back on how you have changed.

Regular practitioners say they develop a feeling of greater emotional equilibrium. In psychoanalytic terms, they involve their egos less in everyday situations. According to Buddhists, one of the results of meditation should be a feeling of compassion – much easier when your ego is dissolved. Self control, in turn, increases self confidence and a person's sense of certainty. Simply put, this means meditation could make you 'nicer' to your fellow beings.

Meditation does not mean 'zoning out'. In fact, regular practice will make your mind sharper and quicker. The ability to concentrate is hugely enhanced, so that tasks take less time and feel easier to accomplish. When you decide to do something, you will be able to just do it, instead of wasting time agonising about it.

On a purely physiological level, meditation has been subject to many scientific studies since the 1960s. These have shown that among its benefits are lower blood pressure, alleviation of some pain, increased levels of the sleep hormone melatonin and lower stress levels. It also seems to help people trying to quit smoking or taking hard drugs. Some doctors have

BENEFITS
- *Confidence and self control.*
- *Inner certainty.*
- *Ability to focus and work efficiently.*
- *Ability to let go of negative emotions such as anger or paranoia.*
- *Relief from insomnia, high blood pressure.*
- *Improved posture.*
- *Greater enjoyment of the physical.*
- *Better personal relationships.*

prescribed meditation for insomniacs, chronic pain sufferers and heart patients, with good results.

However, it is worth knowing that severe depressives and people suffering psychotic illness have been shown in some studies to become worse after practising meditation over a sustained period. If you are concerned about such rare negative side effects you should consult with a medical professional.

RIPPLES OF CALM
Discovering your own inner stillness will have a ripple effect on the rest of your life, bringing surprise benefits as well as some that are more predictable, such as a longer attention span.

The roots of meditation

Who knows how long people have chosen to cease their daily activities for a while and seek inner peace? Quite likely, meditation is as old as the human family itself. Certainly, the roots of modern meditation are found deep in the past. Most religions lay some emphasis on the importance of contemplation and it is within these traditions that we find our techniques. Buddhism and Hinduism, in particular, both have highly developed approaches that everyone can use.

Many Hindu gods are depicted meditating. In particular, Shiva is often shown as a holy man, sitting cross-legged, with eyes half closed, lost in meditation. There is much Hindu literature about meditation; most notably the Yoga Sutra of Patanjali, who was writing some time between 200BC and AD300.

Patanjali explains how to achieve a state that he calls 'samadhi', which translates roughly as total absorption or ecstasy. The methods he describes – breath control, posture, withdrawal and concentration – are the same as those that practitioners of yoga-based meditation use today.

BUDDHISM
Buddha (c. 500BC) reached his goal of enlightenment by meditating for 49 days. Meditating was already common practice for Indian holy men in those days – and Buddha probably used techniques similar to those that have been described by Patanjali. Both religions still share many similar routes to meditation. For example, Buddhists and Hindus may chant a mantra in front of an image such as a thangka from Tibet or a

THE BUDDHA'S MESSAGE
Buddhism helped spread the practice of meditation throughout Asia, as far East as Japan. Meditation is used in Buddhism to help the individual's mind turn inward in order to find enlightenment.

picture of the Hindu goddess Kali.

Buddhism is a religion without a 'God', so Buddhist practice, including meditation, tends to feel especially comfortable for non-believers. Buddha became enlightened using vipassana, one of the simplest and most effective forms of meditation, which focuses on breathing. He taught his followers vipassana and many Buddhists today meditate this way. Since his death, the word of the Buddha has spread and blossomed within different cultures. The result is many schools of Buddhism, which also teach different styles of meditation. There is some common ground between different schools, though. The Buddhist way often involves bringing meditation into everyday life. Buddhists practise mindfulness, which, simply put, means paying attention to the here and now. So if you are chopping a carrot, you focus all of your attention on the chopping of the carrot. This doesn't mean going into a carrot-chopping trance, but simply concentrating fully on the activity. This kind of moving meditation is especially useful for highly active people.

MANDALAS

Since the time of Buddha, devotees have created mandalas as a visual focus for meditation. Mandala means 'circle' in Sanskrit, the Indian language of holy texts. Mandalas are symbolic representations of the order of the universe, often shown as concentric circles populated by deities. The meditator imagines herself travelling through the circles in a spiral to reach the mandala's centre. These works can be

USING YOUR EYES

There are three main ways of using visual aids to help you meditate:

- *Staring at an object, then closing your eyes and recreating the image in your mind's eye.*
- *Gazing at an object without paying attention to it. Whenever you start to have thoughts about it, push them gently away. Try this with an abstract image, such as a yantra (an abstract Hindu mandala) or a Rothko print. Allow yourself to simply 'be with' the image.*
- *Journeying through an image. You can do this with a traditional mandala by starting at one of the gates or you can do this with all manner of other images, for example Tarot cards.*

NOVICE MONKS SAND PAINTING

Novice Buddhist monks (left) create a sand painting of a mandala at Simtokha Dzong.

ephemeral, made of sand intended to blow away, or they may be built to last forever, like the great temple in Java, at Borobodur. The act of creating a mandala is often a form of meditation in itself and usually takes place with some ceremony.

TAOISM AND MARTIAL ARTS

The other great religion of the east, Taoism, also has a long history of meditative practice. Its two most important elements are jing (stillness) and ding (concentration or focus). The goal of Taoist meditation is essentially to circulate and control energy, or chi, within the physical and subtle body. The latter is an integral concept in the Chinese system of medicine.

Many of these Taoist ideas are incorporated into martial arts training. Any martial arts expert will explain that the real power of his or her practice is in the ability to focus the mind. In particular, the 'internal martial arts', Qi Gong, a type of standing meditation, and Tai Chi, which integrates flowing movement with 'one-pointed mind', are highly developed, complex systems of meditation and fitness.

WESTERN TRADITIONS

Christians often meditate – although we may not label what they are doing as such. Contemplation of the images of Christ or the Virgin, telling the rosary, reciting Hail Marys, simply sitting in a church can all lead to a meditative clearing of the mind. The same is true of the other monotheistic religions. The Muslim daily prayers are an exercise in cleansing the mind and

THE MIND'S EYE

This is a concentration exercise called 'tratak', or gazing. It's a classic technique used to help focus the mind and a useful first step on the road to deeper meditative practices.

1. Place a lighted candle at eye level, about 90cm (3ft) away from you.
2. First regulate your breathing, then start to gaze at the candle without blinking.
3. Look steadily and softly at the flame, without straining. If your eyes go out of focus, bring them gently back into focus.
4. When you are ready, close your eyes and keep your inner gaze steady, visualise the object.
5. When the after-image has gone, open your eyes and repeat the process.

focusing on God. Adherents of the Muslim mystical sect of Sufis practise various forms of meditation, including, most famously, whirling, as well as guided visualisations, such as the inner pilgrimage to Mecca.

Part of the Jewish mystical tradition of Kabbalah includes meditating on the tree of life, a visual representation of the path to spiritual enlightenment. The emphasis on language and the actual sound of the Hebrew syllables has interesting parallels with Hindu practice and the use of Sanskrit mantras.

You may want to investigate your own cultural heritage to find aids for your practice. Looking at a rose window may be more meaningful to you than contemplating a Tibetan thangka. You should not feel alienated by any prop you choose for meditation. Whether you have particular religious beliefs, or none, your meditation should not conflict with them.

ROSE WINDOW
Visual imagery can be a good way into meditation. Focusing on the patterns and stories in a stained glass window can be as effective for a Christian as contemplating the thangka is for a Tibetan Buddhist.

THE ROSARY
In the Christian Catholic tradition the rosary serves as a meditation tool for focusing on prayer. Each bead, or series of beads, represents a prayer, so that the person counts them off as he or she prays.

Inward or outward

You don't need to be sitting with your legs crossed and your eyes half closed or surrounded by clouds of incense, in order to meditate. In fact, there's a wide range of meditative techniques, which you will need to choose from to fit in with your circumstances. In different situations, different meditations are more useful. But essentially there are two types: withdrawing and expanding.

WITHDRAWING
In the withdrawing type, the classic yogic meditation, the practitioner blocks out the world by concentrating, for example, on a word or phrase (mantra), a sound, an image or even just their own breathing. The mind is calmed by turning away from the passing caravan of worldly existence and looking inwards at the life of the soul. If you have tried yoga, you may have already experienced this. Once you've mastered ways of withdrawing, you will be able to give yourself a short and intense 'fix' during your day. This is great for releasing tension.

EXPANDING

In the expanding style of meditation, practised by Zen masters, you maintain awareness of what's around you. It means developing your inner 'observer' so you can notice your surroundings and at the same time detach from them. While becoming completely absorbed in what you are doing, you are aware of the world around you. This is the Zen practice of 'mindfulness', a powerful and liberating concept. It's more difficult to master than withdrawing, but eventually expanding can allow you more freedom within your practice.

Body energy

Although meditation is about liberating your mind, you may well find that, at first, you focus on your body in order to achieve that end. Many techniques from Asian traditions involve visualising particular sites on your body.

Eastern wisdom – including traditional Indian and Chinese medicine – conceptualises the body as a system that is constantly pulling in energy and expelling it. For your mind and body to be working at their best you need to be getting rid of stagnant, used up and negative energy, and pulling in positive fresh energy. On a mental level, this is about eliminating negative thoughts and emotions while nurturing positive ones.

Meditations within this framework are, in general terms, about moving the energy within your own system. For example, meditators who build their practice from yoga may work with the chakras, a word which literally means wheels in Sanskrit. The chakra system is a connected series of energy 'wheels' within your body. The Chinese use a similar map of human energy, which is important for Taoist meditation. Whether you view chakras as metaphorical or literal, they can be a powerful tool in meditative practice.

According to most teachers, there are seven chakras – although some would say there is an eighth floating just above your head. They line up along your spinal column and according to the psychically sensitive, they protrude before and behind you. Clairvoyants claim to be able to see the chakras as discs of colour in the body.

WARNING
The effects of serious chakra meditation are strong enough to come with a health warning. Furthermore, you should always do some kind of 'grounding' at the end of a session.

You can access each chakra mentally by visualising it – or physically by doing certain yoga exercises – or even just by massaging the spot where it is centred.

Each chakra is spinning and has a particular colour. Again different sources suggest quite different colours, although currently the most widely accepted range is that of a rainbow, starting with red in the lowest chakra and moving through the spectrum to violet or white in the highest. If you are visualising these colours, these shades should be deep, vibrant and lustrous, as if they are lit from within. However it's unusual to see them all as perfectly mono-hued, after all, one area of life is inclined to leak into the next.

The respected teacher Swami Vishnu Devananda (1927–1993), a pioneer of yoga in the West, recommends two chakras, in particular, for meditators. For those whose approach to life is intellectual, he advises focusing on the third eye, the point between the eyebrows. Those who are more emotional should try focusing on the heart chakra.

If you would like to try dealing with a particular problem, concentrating on the relevant chakra during meditation may release blocked energy. However, this is an advanced technique and the resulting release can be powerful, so it's important that you follow instructions for chakra meditations carefully, and do not omit the final, important 'grounding' part of the exercise (see p.120).

TAOIST PRACTICE

Chinese interest in how energy flows through the human body – how we can conserve good energy and release bad – is reflected in Taoist systems of meditation. One well-known method is to imagine energy flowing into your body through the crown of your head as you inhale; then feel it go right down to a point just below the navel that corresponds with the sacral chakra. As you exhale, you feel the energy shoot back up and out through your crown again.

THE CHAKRAS

Close your eyes to visualise the colours of the chakras. As with all visualisations, everyone will see something slightly different. Some people will clearly see a spinning translucent ball, whereas others will 'feel' rather than see the chakra. Some chakras will seem to be stronger and more active than others – this indicates areas of personal strength. Others may be sluggish or muddy – try focusing on breathing into those chakras to make them come alive.

Crown *Violet*
Spiritual enlightenment,
connection to the source,
transcendence.

Third eye *Indigo*
Second sight, clear thinking,
knowledge, intuition, wisdom.

Throat *Blue*
Communication, openness to
receiving as well as giving
information, self expression.

Heart *Green*
Love, relationships, sharing.

Solar Plexus *Yellow*
Sense of self, boundaries,
assertiveness, will, taking
action.

Sacral *Orange*
Creativity, fertility, making
manifest.

Base *Red*
Connection to the earth,
survival instinct.

Breathing in meditation

There are as many ways to meditate as there are gurus in India – and you should feel free to adopt or reject any of the suggestions. However, whatever meditation you eventually choose to take up, correct breathing and posture are important and useful. If you only learn two things from this book, let it be these. They should eventually become so natural to you that you no longer think about them. Your natural posture and breathing will also improve.

For many of us, controlled breathing provides the easiest gateway into a meditative state. By concentrating on the breath, we can focus inwards into the body and block out the outside world.

LIFE ENERGY
When you inhale you are breathing in fresh energy. It's good to start a meditation by focusing on replacing all the air in your lungs, from top to bottom. With practice, your breathing may become very light once you are into the meditation. According to one study of Tibetan masters, meditating resulted in their needing less oxygen.

BREATH BASICS

There are a few simple rules to remember about breathing during meditation.

■ *Don't forget to breathe.* That sounds pretty obvious, but it's a natural instinct for some people to hold their breath when concentrating. Observe your own breathing and see if you do this.

■ *Breathe through your nose unless directed otherwise.*

■ *Start full.* To begin with, breathe right down into the bottom of your lungs. You may get a head rush from the extra oxygenation, but this will pass as your breathing becomes slow and steady.

■ *Easy does it.* Keep it slow and steady at first. Then as your body relaxes allow your breathing to become more natural and delicate.

■ *Don't gasp for air.* As you get into the meditation your breathing should become more gentle and rhythmic. During deep meditation it should be almost imperceptible, just a delicate rising and falling.

01

02

THE BELLY BREATH

Yoga teaches you how to breathe right down into your stomach, so that your lungs are completely filled with fresh air. This is good to do before you meditate. It involves imagining your lungs in three sections – bottom, middle and top.

(01) Breathe in through your nose, right down to the bottom of your lungs, so that your stomach puffs out.

(02) Exhale, letting your stomach collapse. Do this a few times.

(03) Then do step 1 again, but this time make sure your chest also expands. Exhale, first from the bottom and then from the middle. Do steps 1 to 3 a few times.

(04) Now concentrate on getting breath into your lungs right up to your collarbone. Now you have a full set of lungs. Exhale – bottom, middle, top.

Posture for meditation

There is no one way to sit while meditating, especially since not all methods require being seated. The most important thing is that you feel relaxed and comfortable. However, good posture is really important. It helps with the easy flow of energy, with breathing, and it is ultimately more relaxing for your body – although at first it may not feel like it.

The right posture means having a 'straight' spine. The spine is naturally S-shaped, swooshing forwards from the base and then curving back to the upper back and forwards again to the neck. So if you've been hunching for years, it can be tricky to know whether you're sitting up properly. The easiest way to describe

SITTING UP STRAIGHT
■ *First of all imagine that the top of your head is being pulled towards the ceiling by a string, so that it feels as if your skull is floating on top of your spine. You're like a marionette, dangling.*
■ *Make sure your chin is tucked in. There can be a temptation to throw your chin back.*
■ *Relax your shoulders. Don't pull them back and stick your chest out.*
■ *Make sure your stomach muscles are relaxed. This is very important for your breathing.*

NOTE
You should be sitting correctly now. Remember what this posture feels like, because you will want to come back to it easily if you find yourself slumping during meditation. It should feel comfortable, but it may take you a while to develop the lower back muscles that help you sit up straight.

the sensation of good posture is 'floating'.

The classic position for meditation is the full lotus (see pp.36–7). If you can do it and feel perfectly comfortable in that position, go ahead. Or you may want to sit cross-legged with a cushion just supporting your bottom (see p.35). Try variations on this until you feel comfortable. However, sitting in a straight-backed chair is also fine. The important thing is that your posture is good.

Initially you may want to support your back with a cushion. Eventually you should sit comfortably without a cushion, but bear in mind that meditation should not be an endurance test.

ON A CHAIR

Place your feet flat on the ground. If you're on the short side, you may need to put your feet on something to raise them a little.

MEDITATION POSE ALTERNATIVES

(01) In this version, feet are crossed neatly at the ankles, and the toes touch the ground. Hands rest loosely on the knees.

(02) This version is known as the Full Lotus (see pp.36–7 for detailed instructions). Both feet come up to rest on the thighs and the hands rest lightly on the knees. Hands can be palms up, in one of the mudra positions (see pp.38–9), or palms down. It depends what feels most comfortable for you.

(03) In this Half Lotus position, the top foot rests on the thigh and the hands rest loosely on the knees.

(04) In this version, a simple cross-legged pose is adopted and the meditator is propped up with a cushion under the bottom. This is useful to try if you find sitting cross-legged uncomfortable. Hands rest loosely in the lap.

01

02

03

04

THE LOTUS POSITION

You do not need to be able to do the lotus positon in order to meditate. Most of us just aren't flexible enough and would focus on the discomfort rather than the meditation. However, if you have a bendy body, go ahead and try it.

(01) Sit on a firm cushion or mat on the floor, keeping your back upright. Start with your legs outstretched.

(02) Hold your leg at the ankle in both hands, it doesn't matter which leg you start with. Gently fold it towards the opposite thigh.

(03) Continue folding it towards the top of the opposite thigh, getting it as high as possible.

(04) When your foot is resting on top of the thigh, release and turn your attention to the other leg.

(05) Do the same with your other foot.

(04) Rest your hands on your knees. Choose a mudra that suits you (see pp. 38–9).

01

MUDRAS
Hand positions are called 'mudras' in Sanskrit and they are said to have different effects on your energy. There are quite a few, so you should experiment to see which one you like best. Probably the most relaxed is hands cupping each other (02).

Relaxed (01 & 01a)
The hands rest gently on your legs with palms facing up or down.

Cupping (02)
The right hand is underneath the left and the tips of the thumbs are touching.

Chin mudra (03)
The hands rest on the knees facing upwards with thumb and one other finger (of your choosing) forming an 'O'.

Clasped hands (04)
Calm hands are loosely clasped.

Foundation meditation

Foundation meditation is a basic method based on beginner's Buddhist meditation. Use it as a foundation for your practice. Try it every day for ten or more minutes – the longer the better. You can do it morning or evening, although morning is better as your mind is fresher. At the end of the day you are more likely to drift off to sleep. At first you will probably find that you have trouble letting go of your busy mental process, but persist – anyone can master meditation, even if you have the most hyperactive mind.

After a week or more you should be feeling comfortable – and you should also be able to recognise what meditation feels like to you. Once you know where you are going, you will be able to get

SILENT MEDITATION

(01) Find a comfortable and private place to sit. Be sure that you won't be interrupted for a while. It might be a good idea to take the phone off the hook.

(02) Consciously relax your body all over. Go through each part of your body from top to bottom, thinking about each part in turn. If you feel tension anywhere, you may want to give that

01

there much more quickly and other meditations throughout the day will come more easily. After the first breakthrough, changes come at irregular intervals for most people. Be prepared to reach a plateau of benefit and then unexpectedly move up a notch.

Once you are comfortable with this meditation, you will want to customise it. You may want to start with a ritual, focus on a particular chakra for a week or integrate it with your spiritual practice. The most obvious change you may want to make is the inclusion of a mantra. Some people find that using a mantra means that the process of meditating works much better for them. You may especially want to do this if you find your mind wanders a lot.

02

place a little shake or do a few neckrolls. In particular, make sure your shoulders, stomach and jaw are relaxed. If you are very tense, stand up and shake yourself down. You will find that laughter, if you can laugh 'to order', is the best possible way of relaxing yourself all over.

(03) *When you are ready, close your eyes and focus on your breathing. Focus on the breath as it comes in and out of your nostrils. This is the 'one point' for this meditation. This is where your attention should stay. Take some deep breaths, allowing your stomach to puff out with each inhalation and fall back with each exhalation. Gradually allow your breathing to return to normal. It should be about three seconds in and three seconds out. Some people find counting is a good way to keep focused.*

(04) *You may find that thoughts crowd into your mind. Allow this to happen. You're not supposed to stop thinking when you meditate – just detach from it. Don't push the thoughts away. Try to sit back from them and watch them drift past. When you master meditation you will find yourself in a state of 'not thinking'. If you are overwhelmed by mental activity, return your focus to your breathing.*

(05) When you are ready, come back to full consciousness. You may want to shake out your limbs again.

(06) Try rubbing your hands together. You should feel energised and calm. Now pay attention to how you feel – physically, emotionally and mentally.

GENERAL TIPS
While you are meditating:
- **Don't think about the past or the future.**
You are only in the moment.
- **Don't strain.**
You should be relaxed.
- **Don't be lazy.**
You should be alert.
- **Don't hope.**
Don't have a schedule of expectations. You are not in control. Your meditative practice will unfold of its own accord.
- **Don't be disappointed.**
The benefits of meditation come with persistence.

05

06

Meditation experiences

People report all kinds of different sensations and visions during meditation. But these are not really the goals of the practice. They are, on the whole, just interesting phenomena that you encounter on the way. See them essentially as distractions and remember the ultimate aim of meditation: 'no mind'.

At first, meditation tends to make you more aware of your body as a complete working organism, with blood flowing through your veins, oxygen being exchanged in your lungs and your internal organs working and shifting. This can lead to some odd sensations both internally and on your skin. You may experience tingling and numbness, feel warm and then cold in different parts or all over. You may feel as if you have ants crawling over your skin. You may get a sensation of fullness in different parts of your body. You may feel throbbing. All this is good, you are becoming more aware. Eventually, you will feel as if you have no body at all.

More advanced meditators may start to have visions. At first these may just be colours and light displays on the insides of your eyelids. You may see fireworks, flowers or clouds. Some people see whole landscapes, mansions or temples. All these visions are good; they show that you are deeply in the present moment, which is the essence of meditation. But you should not be seduced by them – they are not the main aim of meditation. So when you have the visions, return your focus to meditating.

SEEING THE LIGHT
If you have a vision of a single white ball of light, then, according to most teachers, you have come through to a high level of meditation. You are close to achieving real bliss. This vision is something on which you can focus. Allow yourself to meld with it.

Dealing with distractions

While you are beginning to meditate, it is easy to become distracted during a session. This can become a bigger and bigger issue, until you are put off the entire practice, so it's important to have some basic techniques for dealing with distractions.

Physical discomfort is a major one. First of all, make sure that whatever position you choose is actually comfortable for you. Although it is important for your posture to be good, there's no point attempting a full lotus position if it causes you any problems.

But even if you are sitting, lying or standing comfortably, you are still likely to feel tingling or numbing sensations in different parts of your body. This is not an endurance test, so gently move the bit that's annoying you just a little, then return your focus to meditation. When it happens again, move a little and then return your attention. By the next time, you should find that you are meditating and any itching or numbness just doesn't bother you. People who meditate for very long periods may move from a standing to a sitting position or even walk around for a bit. The thing is to maintain your inner focus.

Bubbling thoughts are probably the biggest distraction for most people. You start off successfully focusing on your breathing and then suddenly you are thinking about what's for breakfast or what time you need to collect your dry-cleaning. You try to push the thoughts away. Then the floodgates open and you are thinking a whole scramble of thoughts. They seem to be coming thicker and faster than usual.

NATURAL HEALING
Practising meditation out of doors is a time-honoured tradition. The Buddha himself reached his state of enlightenment while sitting under a bodhi tree. Feeling our own connection with the natural world can enhance meditation enormously. If you do have a private space where you won't be disturbed, then use it. If you find yourself being distracted by the sound of leaves rustling or a breeze on your skin, allow yourself to focus on the distraction itself for a while. See it as part of your meditation.

■ Don't try to control your mind. Your mind is boundless and flowing, just like the universe itself.
■ What you need to do is 'sit back' from your thoughts. Don't force them away. Acknowledge them and try not to engage with them.
■ Let the thoughts get smaller and smaller, like tiny boats sailing across the ocean. Soon they will sail over the horizon and you will return to your meditation. Feel patient, because that thought may well come back to bother you.
■ Another way of detaching from your thoughts during meditation is to notice the darkness of your inner eyelids. Notice yourself noticing. You will feel almost as if you are sitting back observing the darkness. Now use that same observer to watch your own thoughts.

FLOATING THOUGHTS
Watch yourself having thoughts. Imagine them drifting through your mind like clouds or balloons across the sky.

- If you need to, you can try exhaling stray thoughts. So imagine that you inhale light and then exhale your unwanted thought.
- Finally, just focus again on your breathing. Come back to your meditation.
- If you feel sleep coming to you, don't fight it, but concentrate on your breathing and try to allow the sleep to brush over your head and behind you. This may sound odd, but try it.
- If that doesn't work, take a few deep, slow breaths, then do a series of about 10 rapid, shallow ones.
- If you are using a mantra (see pp.66–7), say it louder or aloud. Say it faster and then slower. Varying the volume and rhythm will keep you focused.

IMAGINE A FLOATING LEAF
In your mind's eye, imagine a golden leaf in autumn floating away from you down a stream.

CHAPTER TWO

Starting the day

Nothing beats beginning the day feeling fresh, alert and ready for anything. Armed with a few simple meditation tools at your disposal, you should be able to achieve this state easily.

When you open your eyes in the morning, you should awaken with a feeling of joy and anticipation of the day ahead. This is a lot easier to feel if the environment that you see around you is orderly, clear and pleasing to the eye.

When you are making meditation a part of your life, it's important that you create the right kind of ambience in which to practise at home. If you have a family, this can be quite hard to achieve and, at the same time, it becomes even more important to have a particular space that everyone respects.

It's also important to make meditation part of your routine. It should become as integrated into your schedule as brushing your teeth or washing your face. This seems a simple decision, but you may well find yourself putting up mental barriers to implementing a new programme in your busy lifestyle.

If you find yourself making excuses for not keeping a regular meditation schedule, try introducing the process more gradually into your routine. Obviously this slows down the benefits, but it does mean you may eventually integrate it more completely into your life.

When you wake

Some people spring out of bed every morning with a song in their hearts. Most of us find it a little harder to leave the cosy embrace of our bedclothes and face the day. So you'll be glad to find out that one of the general benefits of regular meditation is a feeling of greater alertness when you wake up.

If you find that you suffer from low energy, try starting the day with a 'golden light' visualisation exercise. It's especially useful in winter when your day may actually start in the dark.

Many meditations employ the visualisation of golden light pouring down into the crown of your head or surrounding your body. This light is powerful masculine energy – just the kind that you need to get you through a day at work.

GOLDEN LIGHT
Do this exercise as soon as you are aware that you are awake.

■ *Notice your breathing. Pay attention to how the breath comes in and out of your nose.*

■ *As you inhale imagine pulling golden light in through the top of your head.*

■ *Imagine the light flowing through you with each inhalation – first filling your head, then your throat, then your chest and arms, your waist and finally your stomach and legs.*

■ *Imagine that you are shining with golden light, floating gently just above your bed and radiating beams of light. Stay that way for as long as you like.*

■ *When you are ready, exhale slowly and open your eyes.*

■ *Be sure to eat something after this meditation.*

Establishing a routine

As with any discipline or skill, you need to make meditation part of your ordinary routine. So you need to decide when you are going to set aside your time. Purists will recommend meditating at least twice a day – morning and evening – for 20 minutes a session. But realistically, most of us don't have time for that.

If you can't meditate twice a day, try once a day for 10 minutes – or at least three times a week. Most people have time to brush their teeth and have a hot drink in the morning, so there should be enough time to meditate. But if you're the sort of person who commutes to work in a sleepy daze, gradually waking up after an infusion of caffeine, perhaps meditating when you get back from work would be more fruitful.

ARE YOU A LARK?
If you're an early bird, then meditating with the lark should be no problem.

According to some teachers, the best times to meditate are at dawn and dusk. After you have washed and before you have dressed in the morning, you are especially open to meditation. All meditations are best on an empty stomach and bladder.

You need to be realistic. Only by setting yourself achievable goals will you accomplish anything. A good idea is to take your meditation learning curve on a week-by-week basis. Tell yourself that you will do it every day for a week, then congratulate yourself at the end of that week and set yourself another achievable time period. In this way, you will, almost without noticing, find that you're making meditation part of your daily routine.

...OR AN OWL?
If you are more of an owl and feel alert in the evenings, try to do your meditating at night.

A sacred space

As part of your practice, you should try to create a particular space at home for meditation. It's not essential that you do so, but it helps to put you in the right frame of mind and set your mood. Many people find that as soon as they sit in their special meditation spot they immediately feel calmer.

If you are part of a busy household, the best place to choose may be your own bed. If this is so, you might want to take a little time before starting your meditation to make the bed and tidy your room.

However, if you have the space, try creating a spot dedicated entirely to meditation. It should be somewhere warm and comfortable and the corner of your living room will do. Keep in mind that this space is about helping you to focus your mind inwards, so you should have as few distractions as possible.

If you feel comfortable with the idea, you may want to create an altar on a flat surface at, or just below, eye level – you could use a bedside table, coffee table or a small shelf, for example. This should be a chance for you to express yourself creatively. It's important that you feel that your altar is beautiful – that you have created it yourself, for you. To begin with try to keep your altar reasonably minimal, with only one or two items on display. As time passes, you will add to it and it will develop organically. You might want to add or subtract items to reflect your mood or a special event in your life.

AN ALTAR
Here are some ideas for items you might want to put on your personal altar.

- *Icons, symbols or statues connected to your religious belief.*
- *Candles.*
- *Photographs of family, friends or places that mean a lot to you.*
- *Crystals (but not too many).*
- *Incense.*
- *Flowers or fruit.*
- *Pot pourri or fresh petals.*
- *Something you have created yourself – a painting, a piece of pottery or embroidery, some food.*
- *An altar cloth.*
- *Natural objects you have found – for example, driftwood or beautiful pebbles.*
- *A bell.*

Meditation accessories

As well as the objects on your altar, you may want to include various accessories in your practice. However, it's worth stressing that you don't need tools in order to meditate. They are already within you.

The purpose of rituals and accessories is that with their repeated use you programme yourself to respond to them in a particular way. It's a good idea to put aside special clothes for meditation. These should be loose-fitting and made of breathable material – a silk kimono, perhaps. Get something that's so comfortable that you don't notice you're wearing it. Also wear something that you think is lovely. If this seems excessive, try simply dedicating a shawl to your practice. Many people find that their extremities get cold when meditating, so this can be quite handy.

A live flame is a perfect object for meditation as it is both static and constantly in motion, so invest in a special candlestick for winter morning meditations. Incense can immediately calm an atmosphere, so an incense burner will also be useful.

When you are deciding whether to use particular aids to meditation, you should reflect on what kind of person you are. Which of your senses do you rely on most? Which one gives you the most pleasure?

Most people have two dominant senses and it's useful to know which yours are. Take a little time to think about this. You might want to experiment with some stimuli such as a picture, incense or some simple music. Most people find that they are predominantly a mixture of visual and aural. Tapping into your dominant sense can be an easy entry into meditation.

ATTUNING TO YOUR SENSES

■ *People who are most attuned to sound will benefit from recordings of natural sound – especially the sea or very minimalist music. So you will want to have a CD or tape player in your sacred space.*

■ *Visual people should try using a picture, an icon or a mandala. If you happen to have a window, such as a skylight, which looks out onto sky and nothing else, this can also be a good focal point.*

■ *Smell is a powerful yet very subtle sense and often we are far more sensitive to it than we think. If you meditate using incense try using different scents and see what kind of reaction you have. Try focusing on a particular smell at least once, because you may find that it works surprisingly well for you.*

Creating a ritual

Starting with a ritual begins to create the right context for meditation. The ritual itself will start to put you in the right frame of mind. Like the altar and accessories, this is not a necessary part of learning to meditate, but it will help you integrate the practice into your life. Taking a little time out to formally get into your meditation creates a metaphorical space around the experience – an entry and an exit.

Here are some ideas for physical activities you might like to try before you begin meditating. Choose any of these suggested elements and put them together in an order that suits you.

PHYSICAL EXERCISES

It's not essential to do any physical stretching before you sit down to meditate, but it can facilitate the process. Here are some suggestions, but try to develop your own routine. The exercises should not cause you any physical strain at all, or tire you out.

Neck rolls (01)

Roll your head five times clockwise, then five times anti-clockwise.

Shoulder rolls (02)

Roll your shoulders forwards five times and then backwards five times.

Spine twist (03)

Sitting cross-legged on the floor, twist your torso to the right. Hold your right knee with your left hand and maintain the position until you feel relaxed. Do the same on your left side.

- Do some stretches
- Light a candle
- Burn incense
- Ring a bell
- Place an 'offering' on your altar – food, flowers, a stone
- Rub a pebble
- Touch the objects on your altar

To mark the end of your meditation, exhale slowly and stretch. Reverse (or 'undo') some of the things that you did to begin with. For example, blow out the candle, douse the incense, ring the bell again.

03

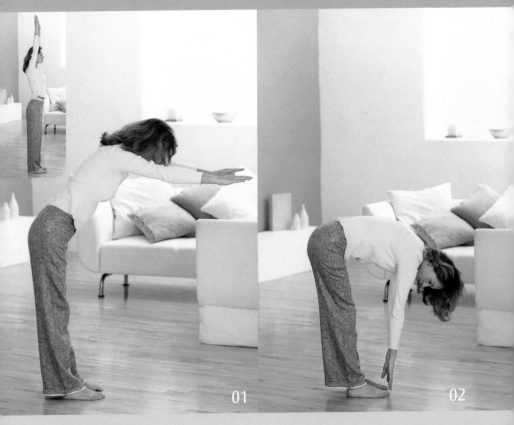

01

02

UNFURLING

(01) Stand with your feet hip-width apart. Stretch your hands above your head as far as you can reach. Then slowly bend forwards, reaching out in front.

(02) As slowly as you can, curl right over until you are touching your toes.

(03) *Then slowly roll back up, leaving your arms dangling at your sides.*

(04) *Your neck should be the last part of you to unfurl.*

(05) *Stand still for a few moments before you move on to your chosen meditation pose (see pp.34–5).*

Pre-breakfast meditation

This is the time to do your main meditation of the day – if you are an early riser.

While you are washing, imagine that you are washing away all your worries and negative thoughts. If you have a morning bath or shower, visualise all that dirty energy going right down the plug hole.

Put on something loose or your special meditation clothes. Either do the standard foundation meditation as outlined on pages 40–43 or try this one with a mantra, which is fantastically energising.

'OM' MEDITATION
This meditation uses the Sanskrit word 'om', the sound of which has an almost magical physical resonance. 'Om' is pronounced 'Ah-oh-mmm'. This is a basic meditation and can be used for other mantras. However, you may want to repeat your mantra silently to yourself instead of out loud. Silent repetition is more difficult.
1. Find a comfortable and private place to sit – either cross-legged or on a straight-backed chair.
2. Check your posture and consciously relax your body.
3. Close your eyes and focus your attention on your breathing. Count four beats, inhaling, hold your breath four beats, exhale four beats, hold four beats. Repeat this six times.
4. On the following exhale, breathe out the word 'om'. Focus your mind on the sound. Repeat 'om' with every exhale. You may find that you sound surprisingly loud to yourself. This is good: just let the sound flow out

'OM'

This is the syllable that the Creator God Brahma is said to have uttered at the beginning of creation – and it still reverberates throughout the universe today. Hindus and Buddhists use it as the most simple and powerful of mantras. Think of it as meaning 'infinity' and simultaneously 'zero' and you will get close to its significance.

naturally. You should start to feel the syllables resonating in your body. The 'mmm' should be vibrating through you. Do six 'oms' and then try six cycles of breathing silently.

5. Check your posture and your physical tension. Relax any muscles that have tensed up.

6. Repeat the cycle again.

7. Don't rush from one 'om' to the next, and remember to keep on inhaling through your nose.

8. When you are ready, come back to full consciousness. You may want to shake out your limbs or rub your hands together. You should feel energised and calm.

Mantras for meditation

A mantra is a special word or a phrase repeated over and over again, in order to clear the mind. It can be done silently, in a whisper or out loud. Both Hindus and Buddhists use mantras in religious practice. The vibrations of the particular words are said to resonate on a spiritual level.

Mantras are only one of the many available tools for the meditator – and not everyone feels comfortable using one. You don't have to have one. For some people the word or phrase itself becomes an unwelcome distraction.

SACRED ARCHITECTURE
Tibetan stupas often contain written mantras. The storage and insertion of the mantras is an important part of their construction. Pilgrims to certain stupas may walk around the building in a clockwise direction reciting a mantra.

But if you are easily distracted during meditation, using a mantra can solve that problem. It is much easier to block out the world around you if you are repeating a mantra out loud. It's also a good way of keeping yourself from drifting off to sleep. If you find yourself getting sleepy as you meditate, you can repeat your mantra louder or faster. People who meditate for very long periods often adjust the speed and volume of their mantra to keep their minds from wandering.

After you've used a mantra for a while, the words become instinctively associated with a state of tranquil meditation. So you can repeat them during your day to keep yourself calm and detached from the hurly burly – even when you are not meditating.

Certain meditation schools suggest that you must be given a specific mantra by a teacher. But others insist that there is no reason why you cannot choose one yourself. You may want to try one of the common Sanskrit mantras. Anyone who has used these can vouch that the sound of the language itself does seem to have a magical resonance. However, you may find it alienating to repeat a word in a language with which you are not familiar.

You could choose words that already have special meaning for you, for example 'Beauty', 'Truth', 'Love' or 'Freedom'. The influential teacher Easwaran Eknath (1910–99) suggested memorising a passage from a mystical text of your choice, for example The Prayer of Saint Francis (see p.135). He uses this as the basis for all his meditative techniques, which are very effective.

'OM MANI PADME HUM'
Hail the Jewel in the Lotus is the most universally used Tibetan Buddhist mantra. The jewel is Buddha himself.

'OM'
The last letter in the Sanskrit alphabet.
(Buddhist, Hindu)

'SHANTI'
Peace
(Buddhist, Hindu)

'SOHAM'
I am that I am
(Hindu)

'OM NAMAH SHIVAYA'
Prostrations to Lord Shiva
(Hindu)

Working up a sweat

You can gain more than a great body by exercising; you will also gain a clearer mind. If you exercise regularly, you know already that you can get into a meditative state when you are at the gym or running through the park. It's just a question of being able to find that particular state every time you try and it's very frustrating when you can't.

Most runners know about a 'runner's high', when certain hormones start to kick in and your feet begin to feel as if they are floating. This is usually accompanied by a feeling of great well-being. That's not what we're talking about here – although the runner's high is a great experience, too.

Repetitive exercise is best for meditation. If you're competing on the squash court or having to second-guess the other team on the football pitch, you'll be spending too much time thinking, which will prevent you from getting into the right meditative state. But going back and forth on the rowing machine, putting one foot in front of the other around the park or lifting weights are all good places to practise a little open- or closed-eyed meditation.

TIPS FOR MEDITATIVE EXERCISE

■ *When you start your exercise, focus on your breathing. Try to keep breathing through your nose. If you can't do that try to keep inhaling through your nose, at least, and exhale through your mouth.*

■ *Focus on your body. Notice which muscles are working and which joints and ligaments are straining. Try to breathe into any place that feels strained. Instead of tensing up as you work out, try to stay relaxed.*

■ *You'll probably find a stream of thoughts coming into your mind. Let them. But try and sit back into your head (metaphorically speaking) and see your thoughts flowing past.*

■ *Watch your breathing and the rhythm of your heartbeat. By the end of your session you should have succeeded in emptying your mind as well as exercising your body.*

CHAPTER THREE

On the move

In the 21st century, many of us spend a lot of time travelling – between work and home, home and the supermarket, holiday destination and home. This 'in-between' time can leave us feeling listless, alienated and drained, but learning to take advantage of 'empty' time can make it something to look forward to.

Waiting is part of being alive – and impatience is part of dealing with the pressures of modern life. We all become accustomed to life moving along at a certain pace and when it doesn't go just as we expect, we can get surprisingly upset.

Travel of any kind involves waiting. We are forced to be patient in the departure lounge, on the train or in line at the check-in. If you stop and look around you next time you travel, it's interesting to see how everyone copes with being forced to wait. Regular commuters have their methods well worked out – a book, a paper, a laptop or even a nap to pass the time. Yet delay that train and it doesn't take long for tempers to rise. Less frequent travellers are often on a shorter fuse and the slightest thing can set them off. But for you, learning to meditate, a delay is an opportunity; being forced to wait gives you precious time.

You can practise meditating anywhere, at any time. Do this on a train, in a waiting room or the back of a taxi. Especially do it if you find yourself getting irritated. As soon as you feel your blood pressure rising, take a breath and let your tension go with your exhalation. Stop your body, check your breathing and allow your mind to clear.

Taking it with you

We invest certain objects with meaning. Sometimes the associations are obvious – wearing a lover's sweater, for example. Doing this consciously is a creative way of bringing peace of mind with you whenever you are on the move.

A smooth stone can be a good personal 'talisman'. Choose a stone that you have found and one that's small enough to carry around in your pocket. If you are using an altar, leave it there for a week or two. Notice it every time you sit down to meditate. Make it part of your meditation ritual, maybe by touching it at the beginning and end of a session. You are building an association in your mind between meditation and the calm that it brings.

You will know when you are ready to take the stone with you. Carry it in your pocket, bag or briefcase – and whenever you're feeling stressed or crowded – on a packed train, for example, hold the stone in your hand. This kind of shortcut works especially well for people who never seem to have a moment to themselves. Even a fleeting moment of calm can de-stress a situation. It works on a subconscious level. The 'sense impression' of the stone recalls the experience of meditation for you.

MEDITATION STONE
Try meditation with your chosen stone, preferably a beautifully coloured smooth pebble, in your cupped hands. Visualise cool, calm earth energy spreading from the stone up your hands and then throughout your body. This should have the effect of making you feel centred and calm. Do this a few times.

Waiting and meditating

If, through meditation, you can learn to actually enjoy waiting, then you will have gained a huge benefit from it. You will start to see periods of waiting as times of opportunity rather than frustration.

Part of what we learn from meditation is being able to let go of our egos, our expectations, our anxieties and just experience existing. Just 'being' is hard, though. It takes practice.

Part of just 'being' is refraining from judging. Think about it and you will realise that wherever you are, whatever you are doing, you spend a certain amount of energy assessing your surroundings, whether it's the people, the sounds, the objects or the smells. You're thinking 'that's nice, that's nasty; she looks capable, he's ugly; it's grey, it's blue'. Try just practising being aware, but without making judgements.

Soften your gaze as you look at objects. Depending on your surroundings you can choose a smell, an object or a sound on which to focus. A smell can be an interesting subject for meditation: easy if you happen to be waiting next to a bakery; hard if you're standing at a bus stop next to a garbage truck.

SNIFF
1. Breathe, relax your body. Allow your eyes to go out of focus.
2. Start to notice the smells around you – and there will be some, both nice and nasty.
3. Notice the tip of your nose and imagine the smell coming in through your nostrils and beginning to float through your body like vapour. With each breath, inhale the smell until you are full of it. Now you and the smell surrounding you are one and the same.
4. If you start to think 'this is horrible' or 'this is lovely', allow the thought in and then let it drift off again.
5. When you're ready, refocus your eyes.

Meditating on the move

'Empty' time crops up constantly when you're on the move – and most of us do a certain amount of travelling every day. Surprisingly, commuting can provide the perfect opportunity for a little quiet meditation. Look around you the next time you are on the train and notice just how many fellow passengers have their eyes shut – yet still seem able to wake up just as the train pulls into their station.

You can do a kind of 'meditation-lite' on the train in order to maintain a certain amount of vigilance. You don't want to go into a deep state only to come back to find your bag snatched. Whenever you meditate you should maintain a certain alertness.

WAITING AT THE STATION
1. Sit or stand, looking out, but slightly down.
2. Take a deep breath and blow out through your mouth. As you exhale, relax your lips, jaw and shoulders. Feel tension sliding out of you; via your mouth, fingertips, the soles of your feet. Let it slip like oil onto the ground and be absorbed.
3. Repeat a few times.

ON THE TRAIN
1. Sit or stand, looking down and slightly to the right.
2. Take a deep breath through your nose and let it out very slowly. Do this a few times and consciously relax. If you're standing, bend your knees a little.
3. Listen to the train's rhythm.
4. Feel the movement through your body. Sway round corners.
5. Keep breathing. Stay relaxed. Notice your body.
6. Feel the heat that your own body generates all around you and a short distance from your body.
7. Get off at your station.

Walking meditation

Zen walking meditation, or 'kinhin', was developed as a way to take a break from sitting meditation, but it works well in its own right. If you have to walk a short distance every day, say to the train, to the shops or around campus, use kinhin as a starting point for developing your own meditation method. You probably don't want to draw attention to yourself, so you can adapt kinhin for ordinary walking.

KINHIN

(01) Stand with feet hip-width apart. Shake out your body. Make sure your back is straight and your chin is tucked in. Start to pay attention to your breathing.

(02) Make a relaxed fist with your left hand and put it over your heart. Cup it with your right hand. Let your elbows drop down and your shoulders relax. Keep breathing.

(03) Look down to the ground just in front of you. Relax your gaze.

(04) While inhaling, slowly lift your left foot, heel first. Peel it off the ground and take one small step.

(05) Exhaling, press your left foot down slowly, heel first. Do the same sequence with your right foot. Pay attention to every movement you make and keep your breathing in sync with your footsteps.

01

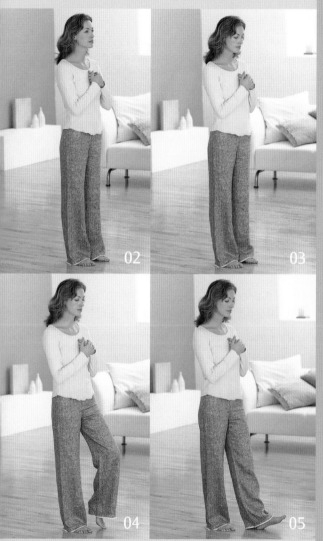

Variations
Try taking longer steps, maintaining synchronous breathing and stepping. Pay attention to every part of your body, keeping loose and relaxed. Notice your knees, your hips, joints, the way your arms move, the shift of weight from right to left, the feeling of air moving past your body.

Long-haul meditation

You would hardly think that being stuck in a plane for hours was the ideal time to practise meditating. But, when you're on a long-haul flight, you have to be calm and you have to relax – otherwise the whole experience becomes an endurance test.

You can adapt some of the other meditations in the book to suit this situation. Try the goodnight meditation on pages 124–5, if you are trying to sleep. To take advantage of your airborne state try the visualisation on this page and develop it. Imagine the world beneath or you as a spaceman floating past the rings of Saturn. Remember to keep breathing.

CLOUD 9

1. Make sure you're comfortable. Loosen your clothes; kick your shoes off. If you're a shortie, support your feet with a footrest or pillow.

2. Relax, breathe gently, close your eyes.

3. Lean your head on the backrest, drop your shoulders.

4. As you inhale, imagine pale, translucent light pouring in through your third eye (at your brow) and filling your body.

5. As you exhale, imagine darkness flushing out of your body – yes, from your bottom.

6. When you feel that the dark has left you and you are quite filled with light, try to imagine that the plane is no longer surrounding you. Instead, you are floating on a cloud or even in the clear blue sky. If it's a night flight you may be surrounded by stars. Feel the air supporting you and the wind caressing your temples.

Meditation in transit

There are two contrasting meditations to try when you are travelling. One is a way of letting go (Nothing Meditation, right) and the other is a way of staying centred (Traveller's Altar, far right).

LETTING GO

According to Buddha, the road to enlightenment begins with letting go of earthly attachments – home, family and possessions. We need to stop desiring things – a big car, respect, even love – and learn to see that the life we lead in this material world is illusory. These are hard concepts, but once grasped, however fleetingly, they can set your mind free. 'Letting go' means letting go of everything, and this is easier when you are in transit. Hotel rooms are great places to contemplate the transitory nature of our lives, the scale of our possessions and the unfixed nature of emotions. However, letting go is not for everyone, as losing a sense of your roots and grounding can be destabilising. Be aware of yourself and what kind of person you are before trying the Nothing Meditation.

STAYING CENTRED

If anonymity and nothingness make you feel uneasy, you may only really be able to relax if you can take a little piece of home with you. If this describes you, then acknowledge it. Most of us need to feel grounded in order to feel safe and so losing your sense of yourself and your centre can leave you vulnerable when you are away from home. If you feel exhausted, drained and disoriented, then try it.

NOTHING MEDITATION
This exercise can leave you feeling exposed and unprotected, so do it just before going to sleep.

*1. Put all your possessions away in the wardrobe so that there's nothing in the room to remind you of 'you'.
2. Have a bath or shower.
3. Sit on the edge of the bed or cross-legged in the middle of it and do your usual meditation.
4. Once you are relaxed try and focus your mind on the idea of 'om' – zero and infinity. Repeat the word silently for a while.
5. Imagine your mind expanding into space, so that you and space become as one. You may find this hard or easy. It may be fast or slow. Stay with it. If you have difficulty, imagine that your mind is slowly expanding outwards with each exhalation.
6. When you are ready, inhale and pull yourself back to your body. This may take several inhalations.*

TRAVELLER'S ALTAR

You only need one little object to create your own mini-altar in your hotel room. Bring something from home that you normally see or touch every day – a figurine, a stone, a shell, a perfect chestnut, even a postcard will do. All you need is something that comforts you, on which to focus your attention. Then you can do your normal daily meditation.

EARTH CONNECTION

(01) Take a bath or a shower and as you sluice away the water imagine all the negative energy of the day washing down the plughole.

As you step out, inhale and feel your body lighten. Let your shoulders drop, and start to focus on your breathing as you walk into the bedroom.

Stay standing and place your feet a hip-width apart. Count your breathing – four beats in, hold four beats, four beats out, hold four beats and then round again.

After a few cycles, move your focus to the soles of your feet and feel the way they are touching the ground. Try to feel each toe individually, sinking into the ground.

Slightly bend your knees and feel yourself sinking into the ground a little.

(02) Bring your hands in front of you, one above the other, as if you are holding an invisible ball. Hold the ball just below your navel. Keep breathing.

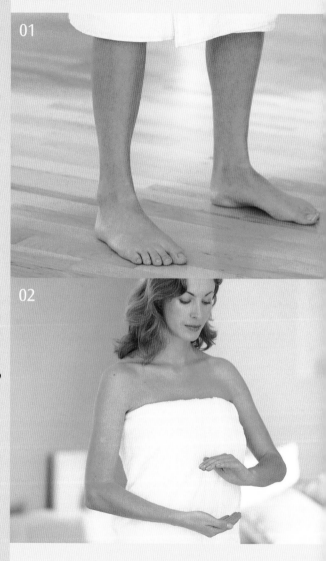

01

02

(03) Gently move your hands further apart and closer together. You will feel energy between your hands as a slight, warm resistance. Feel the energy running down your spine and straight into the ground. It's like a pillar of light connecting you to the earth. Hold this posture as long as you feel comfortable. Keep your mind focused on your physical body – how your feet feel, the warmth between your hands, your breath, the space between your tailbone and the floor.

(04) Don't stand so long that you start to feel stressed. When you've finished, imagine the column of light telescoping back into your body. Shake out your limbs.

03

04

At work

Your work – whether merchant banker or mother of two, or both – can present more challenges to your inner tranquillity than anything else you do. Learning how to relax during your working day deals with the stress as it comes to you, so that you don't carry it into the evening or the next day.

One of the effects of regular meditation is to clear your mind. This means you can work in a concentrated, lucid manner without getting distracted by details or confused by conflicting opinions.

During your working day, you may come across challenges, perhaps in relation to colleagues, that are best tackled in a cool, calm and collected manner – instead of dealt with in a rush of adrenaline. Taking a little time to meditate before taking action will help you to take a more detached approach.

Apparently, we are all working longer hours, with fewer breaks, than ever before. According to statisticians this is accompanied by decreasing productivity. The lesson of this could well be that claiming time for yourself during your working day not only benefits you personally, but also helps you do your job more efficiently.

Work is a time when you can put into practice certain 'instant' meditation techniques. These quick fixes should be based on the routine meditation that you are practising at home.

The right environment

You may be lucky enough to have an understanding employer or be running your own show. If so, think about setting a room aside for meditation – or at least using a room at a particular time for the purpose.

If you can get a group of like-minded colleagues together, meditating in a group is a great way to keep up your own meditation programme. Often the energy of group meditation is powerful enough to enhance your own concentration. However, most of us are living in the current age rather than the 'New' one, so aquiring a meditation room at work might be just a far-fetched dream. You will need to make your own arrangements. Find somewhere where you won't be

ZAZEN

Zen Buddhists practise a form of meditation called 'zazen', which involves gazing gently at something neutral such as a blank wall, or the ground in front of your feet. It's a great way to blank out distractions when you're in an otherwise busy environment.

disturbed – a boardroom or stockroom, perhaps. Really, all you need are peace and quiet. But if you can manage it, a place with dim light is good and not too much visual distraction.

The next best thing to a special room at work is meditating outside. If you leave your work environment for a while and find a different space, your daytime meditation will be more refreshing. Being outside is more distracting, however. Failing both alternatives, learn to meditate at your desk or on the hoof. Like any skill, this requires a bit of practice, but long term it's more useful since you will learn to meditate anywhere.

Your work space

People like to decorate their desks with things that remind them of home and family, holidays and happy memories. By all means do this, but keep part of your work space for contemplative materials. Here are some suggestions.

To the right of your desk pin a postcard or drawing of something that you consider spiritually intriguing – a rose window, the Virgin Mary, a Tibetan thangka, a native American medicine wheel, a mandala or an Indian yantra. Choose a picture that strikes a chord with you – it may be simple or very elaborate. If you're artistic, you might want to make your own drawing.

Straight ahead of you, pin a picture of a tranquil landscape in which you'd like to imagine yourself. Whenever you feel work oppressing you, practise visualising yourself in that landscape, with its particular weather, smells and sounds.

If you are a sensual type, something you can touch will be appealing. Bring a natural object such as a stone, a crystal, a piece of bark, a shell, a dried flower and keep it in your top drawer. Don't leave it on your desk as you need to keep its associations undiluted.

TRANQUIL TUNES
An excellent aid to office meditation is your own private headset, though naturally this should not interfere with your work. Choose natural sounds or even white noise to block out the world around you. Or you could make a recording of yourself talking through a visualisation.

YANTRAS
These are abstract geometrical mandalas in the Hindu tradition. They are used as a visual focus for meditators. The most well-known is the shri yantra, which shows the meeting of the masculine and feminine force, represented respectively by upward- and downward-pointing triangles. Hindus may also use the image of a god or goddess as the departure point for meditation.

Intention and attention

The best way to carry out any work, whether at home, at the office, or out and about – mundane or heavy-weight – is with complete mindfulness – that is, with all the attention and concentration you can muster and a sense of living one hundred percent in the present. This involves working with 'intention'. Then you will find the task relaxing, rewarding and even joyful. It will certainly be creative.

For some jobs, depending on your character, that's easy, but all of us sometimes have to do things we dislike or would simply rather not tackle, and here's the real challenge for our new-found meditative skills.

HARD WORK

■ *At the beginning of a particular task – the more onerous the better – tell yourself that you will give it your complete attention. If it's something truly hideous, give yourself an achievable time limit, say, 20 minutes. So, close your eyes for a moment, take a breath and tell yourself, 'I am going to give my complete attention to doing the accounts [for example] for 20 minutes and then I'm allowed a break.' You may have to do a lot of 20-minute chunks in order to complete the task, but you will find that you can go for longer and longer periods, until eventually you don't have to give yourself an incentive.*

■ *Then do your job with complete mindfulness. Every time your mind strays from the task in front of you, bring it gently back, just as you would in meditation.*

■ *Think of your work as being rather like climbing a steep hill. You need to set an easy pace that won't over-stretch you. If you concentrate on each step as you take it, making sure that it is the most perfect step, that your weight is beautifully distributed, that it is easy to manage, then suddenly you arrive at the crest of the hill.*

■ *Before you know it the task is done and you have an enormous sense of achieve-ment. Perhaps it was even fun, too.*

Before a challenge

A certain amount of tension is good before a challenge such as an interview or an exam. You want to be fully alert and attentive to each and every question. However, being too tense has the strange effect of making your mind wander. If you are very stressed out, you will find it difficult to focus. Your mind will drift off and you may even lose the thread of a conversation – not very impressive!

When you need to calm down quickly, try some yogic breathing. In the yogic tradition, controlled breathing is known as 'pranayama' and it is always practised before meditation. Inhaling pulls in prana, the life force, and exhaling gets rid of negative energy.

SWEET BREATH
This exercise is worth having in your arsenal of handy meditations. Ten rounds of this should calm you completely. Count to four for each step in the cycle.

(01) With your left hand, put your thumb over your left nostril, fold your first two fingers into your palm.

(02) Put your ring finger on your right nostril.

(03) Close your left nostril with your thumb and inhale through your right nostril.

(04) Close your right nostril and exhale through your left. Inhale through your left.

(05) Close your left nostril and exhale through your right.

LEFT AND RIGHT
A clear left side shows that your right brain (creative thinking) is flowing well; a clear right side shows the left brain (logical thinking) is working well.

01

Activating your chakras

If you want to activate a particular kind of energy – say creative energy – through meditation, it's useful to understand the chakra system (see p.131). Chakras can be activated both with physical movements or by visualisation.

There are many different ways of activating the chakras and you will find as you develop awareness that you will modify and refine methods that work best for you. Taking a physical approach to chakra awareness is a good way of switching off your mind. You concentrate on the movement so much that you forget everything else.

01

CHAKRA SHAKE-OUT
If you need to use your creative imagination and communicate, activate your top three chakras – throat, third eye and crown. This exercise should be done quickly.

(01) Sit correctly and breathe easily. Focus attention on your blue throat chakra. Roll your head three times to the right and three times to the left.

(02) Focus on your indigo third eye chakra. Tilt your head to the side, stretching your neck as far as possible. Do the same thing in the other direction.

(03) Next focus your attention on your violet crown chakra. Snap your head twice to the left, then twice to the right; bend twice to the left, then twice to the right.

(04) Snap your head twice backwards.

(05) Then nod twice, stretching your spine. Now you're ready for work!

Avoiding confrontation

One of the lessons of meditation is discovering an inner 'observer', the part of you that simply watches what is going on without judging or becoming emotionally engaged. You need to find this observer part of yourself in order to deal with distractions during meditation. If you can find it again, when you are dealing with a tricky situation at work, you will find it very useful and be able to take a more detached view of the problem.

Most of us are not lucky enough to be staying at a retreat or living in an ashram: you just don't have time to go into a deep meditation during the day. The best you can do is rest and refresh your mind briefly. If you find yourself in a situation that's getting out of hand, see if you can take a few moments on your own to do the yoni mudra on pages 104–5.

But in many situations, say during an important meeting, you will be under too much pressure to be able to stop and meditate, so you need to have some detachment exercises that are already 'programmed' into your consciousness. Try working on these at home, and you will have an imaginative toolkit to call on whenever you need it.

RECALLING TRANQUILLITY

■ *After you have finished an ordinary meditation at home, spend some time paying attention to how you feel, both physically and mentally. You don't have to put these feelings into words – simply notice them.*

■ *When you have finished take three short breaths in through your nose, hold for a moment and then let go gently. As you do so tell yourself that you will remember this feeling of relaxation and whenever you take three breaths like this, you will return to this state.*

■ *This may not work at first, but repeat the exercise when you meditate at home and then practise your three breaths during the day. You will find that eventually you have made the connection between the breaths and a state of calm.*

01

02

A ROOM IN YOUR MIND

Try creating a room in your mind to which you return in order to relax and detach. Put as much imaginative effort and detail into creating this room as you can – you want your room to become part of your imaginative toolkit. You can then conjure it up quickly when you want to retreat to a safe place in your mind.

(01) Prepare yourself for meditating as usual, but keep your eyes open.

(02) Sometimes it helps to look up and to the right.

03

(03) *Imagine there is a room in your head and you are sitting in the room looking out of your eyes. What's the room like? Maybe it's cool and minimalist, maybe it's cosy and warm. Furnish it as you please. It should feel tranquil and safe. When you are ready, bring your attention back.*

Lunch-time meditation

Your lunch hour may be the only time you have to yourself during your working day. Cherish it. Don't waste precious time eating lunch hunched at your desk or snacking over a game in cyberspace. Make the most of your time by practising a quick, intense meditation that clears the mind, ready for the rest of the day. Usually, it's best to meditate before a meal rather than after, but if you are famished it may be better to eat first so you're not distracted.

Ideally, go to a park or at least a bench outdoors. Being with nature is an easy way to enhance your experience and will give you something absorbing on which to focus.

MIDDAY MEDITATION
Adapt this meditation to suit your surroundings and circumstances. A fountain or pool is an ideal focus. If you can, give yourself a clear quarter of an hour to complete it.

(01) Sit up straight, with your spine aligned and your feet flat on the ground. Either close your eyes or look at moving clouds, flowing water or a sunbeam; anything that suits you. Don't focus your eyes. Allow the clouds or water to move across your vision. Soften your shoulders and your throat. Pay attention to your breathing. Breathe gently through both nostrils. Allow your breath to be light and sweet.

01

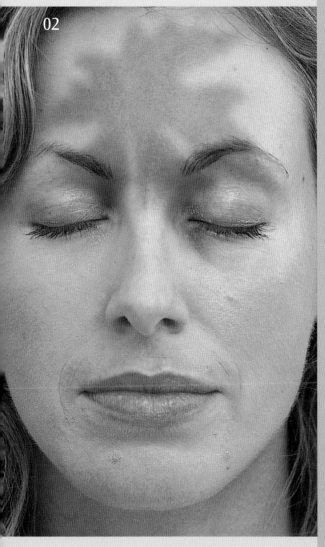

02

(02) Now bring to the front of your mind anything that's been bothering you during the morning. If your eyes are closed, visualise your worry as a leaf blowing in the wind and let it drift away. Do the same thing with any other worries. If your eyes are open, put your worry on the cloud or float it on the water and watch it drift away. Now rest in the empty space at the front of your mind. When you are ready, return to full consciousness.

Meditate – concentrate

Sometimes a working day can seem like an assault on all five senses – which makes it very difficult to concentrate if you need to get that report finished or that invoice accurate. If you have an urgent task that requires your undivided attention for the morning or afternoon, try this intense yogic exercise. This will help you block out all the unnecessary information that's bombarding your mind and focus on the task at hand.

YONI MUDRA

The Yoni Mudra is an exercise in short-term sensory deprivation – a lot cheaper than a flotation tank. It should leave you feeling calm, clear and ready for the next challenge.

1. Find somewhere where you won't be disturbed for a few minutes. Sitting in a toilet cubicle is fine.
2. Focus on your breathing.
3. Close your ears with your thumbs.
4. Shut your eyes with your index fingers.
5. Close your nostrils with your middle fingers – allowing breath in and out, of course.
6. Shut your mouth with your ring fingers and rest your little fingers on your chin.
7. Focus attention on your breath rushing in and out of your nose.
8. Let go of your nostrils, inhale for four beats. Close your nostrils and hold for four beats.
9. Let go of your nostrils and inhale.
10. Repeat your breathing cycle ten times.

Energise – meditate

Some time in the middle of the afternoon most of us are ready for a quiet siesta. However, most offices don't come equipped with a comfy chaise longue – and most employers won't give you time off for a kip.

To boost your energy, you could try visualising a ball of fire just below your diaphragm, which gradually spreads its hot energy throughout your body. Taking a short walk away from your desk will also help.

THE PURPOSE OF BREATH OF FIRE
The Breath of Fire will fill you with hot, life-giving energy. This is the kind of feeling you need before getting stuck into any kind of job, especially if it requires physical strength or creative power.

01

02

BREATH OF FIRE

(01) Sit or stand in a good easy posture. Close your eyes if you like, but it's not strictly necessary. Start to breathe normally and make sure your whole body is relaxed. In particular, relax your jaw and throat.

(02) Inhale through your nose and then snap your diaphragm up to exhale, shooting out a short breath. Inhale again and snap your diaphragm up again. Do this a few times until you think you have mastered the technique. Then go for it and do 20 or so breath cycles in a row. Breathe normally again and then do another group of short breaths.

NOTE

If you feel dizzy after this exercise, check your posture and breathing and keep to just one group of 20 cycles.

Leaving work behind

Creating a little ritual for leaving work makes it easier to leave mental or emotional messes behind at the end of the day, and start with a fresh slate for the evening ahead.

You will need to go through this ritual a few times before it starts to have any effect. When you first do it, you will need to think about it, but what you want is for the ritual to become automatic, so that you can switch off your mind and go into a meditative state.

RITUAL DEPARTURE

■ *First of all, pay attention to your breathing and start to breath into your abdomen. Consciously relax your body. Now go about your business, continuing to breathe without holding your breath.*

■ *Tidy up your work area. If you are one of nature's slobs, don't worry, this is 'ritual tidying', which means that you should choose, say, three things, that always have to be put back in the same place in your workspace – for example, a pen, a mousemat and a notepad – or a chisel, a screwdriver and a can of oil. As you put each object back in its place, tell yourself that you are leaving work behind.*

■ *This may seem a strange concept, but try to let go of any energy connection you have with your work tools. As you put each item back, imagine that you are reeling back energy into your hands and away from the tools.*

■ *Now pack your bag and put your coat on. As you shut your bag, exhale. Work is being left behind. As you put*

your coat on, imagine work pouring off it onto the floor. Step over the puddle you've left behind.

■ *As you walk through the door, exhale and imagine that you are leaving a whole slew of work energy behind. It's pouring off you. As you step out the door, imagine a blast of light showering down onto you and giving you energy. Inhale this light and keep walking.*

NOTE
You should feel work-free and energised by this little visualisation. If you've had a particularly sticky day, intensify this meditation. Really focus in on it. Like all visualisation, it becomes more powerful the more you practise it.

CHAPTER FIVE

Learn to relax

The most important thing this book can do for you is teach you how to let go of your worries and relax. If you know how to relax, life will open up for you, and you will find more moments of happiness within each day than ever before.

By letting go of tension, you are making room for good things to come into your life. By clearing your mind, you are making room to appreciate the beauty and strangeness of the world.

We often make the mistake of postponing relaxation. 'I'll just get through this week,' you say to yourself, 'and then it's my holiday and I'll really wind down'. And sure, you manage to relax by the second week of the holiday, but then the following Monday you're back at work and it's as if you'd never been away.

You need to learn to relax whenever you choose to – whether it's for a micro-second during a busy day – or for a long, well-earned break. You can do this by integrating meditation into your normal schedule, but also by importing some of your holiday mood into your everyday existence.

Switching off

Our days are spent thinking, acting and reacting. Our minds are constantly alert, ticking away like little clocks. Try stopping the clock for a moment every now and then and switching off.

The key to meditation is learning to deal with distractions. You can only do this by practising, so take every opportunity to do so. During an average day, you will have many moments of downtime – waiting for the kettle to boil, standing in the bus queue, buttering the toast, in the shower. For the next week, try this exercise: just stop.

JUST STOP
Each time you do this exercise, you will find that you relax completely, if only for a few moments. So you are giving yourself more time this week during which you are totally relaxed. If you're a highly stressed individual, you should feel a huge difference by the end of the week.

1. Stop what you're doing. That's right – freeze.
2. Let your vision drift out of focus.
3. Breathe into your belly. Now breathe normally, but keep the cycle of breath going.
4. Relax your shoulders, relax your mouth and jaw.
5. Let your thoughts drift away from you. You are a rock and nothing more.
6. Stay immobile as long as you can.
7. Now get on with what you were doing.

Welcome pleasure

It's important at the start of the weekend or at the beginning of a holiday to leave as much of your daily grind behind as you can. Take your personal well-being seriously so that you're primed to totally enjoy the good times ahead. If you make a morning meditation part of your Saturday routine, you can start the weekend on a positive note. Get up at dawn – if you possibly can. According to some gurus, the time just before and just after the sun comes over the horizon is the optimum for meditating. All over the East, people go to temples at dawn and say their prayers or meditate. In the West most of us have lost

SATURDAY MORNING DETOX

Get up at dawn and do this meditation before you eat anything. Sit outside or in front of a window. Keeping your eyes slightly open, start to meditate in your usual way – with the right posture and breathing, focusing in, clearing your mind and relaxing your body. When you feel relaxed and beginning to flow in meditation, start to repeat this phrase aloud or silently, 'Let in the light'. As you do so, feel you are breathing the daylight through all your pores. Continue for as long as you like.

the connection with the natural rhythm of the day, but if you can find it at the weekend that's good.

On holiday, most people find that it takes at least three days before they stop thinking about what they are escaping from. By the end of the first week, you are probably into a routine and absorbed by your surroundings and new experiences.

In an ideal world, you will have been able to meditate on your journey, letting go of home-based worries. Even so try this meditation for letting go. The more you can let go at the beginning of your holiday, the more room you make for new stuff to happen.

RECLAIMING YOURSELF

This is a visualisation about reclaiming all the energy you have expended on other people over the week. It can also be good after a particularly tiresome day.

1. Prepare for meditating. Sit, close your eyes, regulate your breathing.

2. Think about the projects, people and problems that have claimed your attention and energy during the week. Visualise a cord of energy running from your body to each of these issues.

3. When you are ready, imagine that you are pulling in all the energy that you have put out over the last week. With each breath reel in the energy as if it were on a fishing rod. Some energy will come back easily and some will take several breaths to reel in.

4. At the end, open your eyes and have a glass of water.

5. You should now feel enormously uplifted.

[This meditation is included courtesy of Nina Ashby.]

Holiday magic

The end of a holiday is bound to be sad, as you brush the sand off your feet for the last time or put away your ski boots.

Let's hope you've had a wonderful holiday – full of magical moments. You're feeling younger, better-looking, more intelligent and generally terrific. How can you hang on to this feeling?

The truth is, you can't. Everything changes; everything moves on. But when you are back at home, you can consciously recall your holiday feeling whenever you've got the blues.

The following exercise is a form of category meditation, a method which is sometimes used to teach beginners. Some people, very visual types, find this the most effective means of achieving 'one-pointed mind'. If you find that neither meditating with a mantra nor the basic breathing meditation are working for you, try category meditation (see right) as your basic morning workout. It is especially good for improving your ability to visualise and you can adapt this to fit any situation.

You will need to think of four different types of the same thing. The classic example is flowers. In this case, choose objects that are connected with your holiday. Four different tropical fish, for example, four shells or four church doors. The possibilities are endless, but they must appeal to you aesthetically.

CATEGORY MEDITATION

■ *Once you have settled into your meditation, in your mind's eye, imagine the first of your objects. You may want to put it in context: the various flowers in the four corners of a garden, for example. Look at one of the flowers in detail. Examine each pistil and stamen. Be meticulous in your observation. When you have thoroughly examined the first object, do the same with the next three.*

■ *You will have fixed these objects in your mind now. Whenever you want to get into a meditative state, think of them.*

HOLIDAY MEDITATION

If you go on holiday to a very beautiful place, somewhere tranquil and safe, use it for your meditation.

■ *Choose a particular spot and sit there for a while. Look at everything around you in detail. Take your time to memorise each rock, each blade of grass, the way the water splashes into a pool or the sun filters between pine needles. Try to absorb the place visually. Drink it in with your eyes. Breathe it in with your lungs. Sniff it. Touch it. Listen to the sounds around you – birdsong, waves, wind or cicadas.*

■ *Take your time because you are creating a care package to use on your return home. This place will be somewhere you go to in your head, so the more detail you can create now, the better. You may want to keep visiting the place during your holiday or you may be satisfied with just one visit.*

■ *Back home, use your holiday spot as a mental retreat. Recall it often, perhaps during daily meditation, so that it becomes part of you.*

Chakras and meditation

Getting to know the chakra system takes commitment (see also pp.26–7). So it's a good idea to put aside some concentrated time, perhaps while on holiday, when you can work on them consecutively. Consider most chakra work as advanced and only attempt it if you have plenty of time and private space.

Meditating with chakras requires a leap of faith. The idea at the basis of chakra work is that you are getting the energy in your system flowing smoothly. This means that you want to release blocked energy, but you don't want energy whizzing through your system too quickly. A chakra that spins sluggishly or not at all will manifest as an emotional or material problem in the area of its association. For example, someone with a blocked throat chakra may have trouble making themselves heard. People may ignore him or he may literally have a frog in his throat. On the other hand, a person whose throat chakra spins too fast may talk too much. Either way, there's an imbalance.

Only you can tell which chakras need work. Once you are used to the idea, you can give yourself a chakra check-up occasionally. Visualise each chakra in your mind's eye. If it's the size of a grapefruit, spinning fairly fast, has good clear colours with nice smooth edges, then it's OK. Most people find that some chakras are always strong while others vary. It's quite common to find that the upper chakras are fine while lower ones need work, or vice versa. If you find your upper chakras are always stronger, you should be careful with any physical activity after working on them. For example, driving can be tricky.

FULL CHAKRA MEDITATION
This is a full-on visualisation, which should leave you feeling highly energised.

1. Sitting comfortably, close your eyes and start to focus in on your breathing.
2. When you are feeling calm and centred, begin to visualise a lustrous ruby chakra spinning at the base of your torso. You may find that what you see in your mind's eye is not a perfect red – don't worry.
3. Imagine this chakra for as long as you like, then move on to the sacral chakra. Do the same with each one, moving up the body and finishing with the crown chakra. Try to visualise each spinning freely. You may find that the chakras you imagine are rough or wobbly. Try getting them to run smoothly. Let your mind's eye repair them.
4. After you have finished visualising the crown chakra, try imagining all of your chakras spinning at once.
5. Imagine a clean current of violet light snaking down

through your chakras from
above the crown and straight
into the ground.
6. Let any negative energy
out through the root chakra.
Feel positive energy coming
in through your crown
chakra.
7. When you are ready, open
your eyes. You should feel
highly energised.
8. Now it's time for
grounding. Choose the
method that most suits you.

WAYS OF GROUNDING

Drinking a glass of water.
Having something to eat.
Having a shower.
Stamping your feet.
Having a catnap.

Sexual healing

Sex is just one part of the Indian mystical tradition known as 'tantra'. But it is the part that tends to get the most attention. A key ritual in tantra is known as maithuna, meaning 'union' in Sanskrit. This is 'meditative sex' – you focus 'one-pointed mind' (see p.6) on union with the other person.

Have a bath or shower and get squeaky clean. If you have a bearskin rug in front of an open fire, then lucky you: do your tantric sex there. However, a big, firm bed is a pretty good place for making love any time of day. Maithuna requires patience and space, so allow plenty of time. It will improve with repetition, so try giving yourself a time once a week for a tantric love-in.

LOOK OF LOVE
1. Sit facing, just touching at knees or fingertips, and look into each other's eyes.
2. Start breathing in unison. Take deep belly breaths, through the nose first and then naturally.
3. Keep looking into your lover's eyes. Allow your gaze to melt in and out of focus. If attention wanders, bring it gently back to the eyes.
4. Visualise your darling's third eye as a glowing light. Can you feel your own? Imagine these two points exchanging energy.
5. Gently touch the other's face. Focus on the touch – on the tips of your fingers and the sensation of your lover's skin. Take your time.
6. Stroke each other gently. You'll want to move around now, into whatever position seems comfortable. The man should stroke the woman's right side first and the woman should stroke his left. Put all your attention into the touch. Keep breathing in unison.
7. Now progress to full love-making, or stop.

THE STAR

*You may want to move on to
full lovemaking. In the
tantric star position, the
man sits cross-legged and the
woman sits astride him with
her legs around his waist.
1. The woman should mount
the man in the star position
and allow him to penetrate
her deeply.
2. Look into each other's eyes
and breathe in unison.
Without moving, focus on
your first chakra.
3. Your chakra and your
partner's should meld into
one ball of energy – like a
single red ball of fire,
vibrating. Keep in this
position as long as you can.
4. Gradually, you may feel
energy travelling up your
spine from the root chakra.
5. Allow this energy to flow
through all your chakras and
out through the top of your
head. If it's not automatic,
visualise the rising together.
6. When you're both ready,
you may want to start
moving. Keep it slow and
focus in on every sensation.
The goal of tantric sex is not
orgasm, but union.*

Good night

Once you have started to reduce your daily stress levels, you will find that sleep comes to you more easily and you sleep more profoundly. You may also need to sleep for fewer hours per night, since you will have become less exhausted during the day. Furthermore, you should wake up from the sleep you have feeling well rested.

For the regular insomniac these are big promises. But it's worth noting also that bouts of insomnia are good times to practise meditation. Instead of pacing the house or looking at the contents of the fridge at two in the morning, use that time to practise. Try meditating yourself to sleep.

PUTTING YOURSELF TO SLEEP

Although it is not meant to send you to sleep, you can use meditation techniques to put yourself to sleep. Try this as you are lying in bed in the dark, waiting for sleep to come.

1. Lie comfortably, with arms at your sides and legs uncrossed. Breathe normally.
2. Say to yourself, 'toes go to sleep' and consciously relax your toes. Then say, 'feet go to sleep' and do the same. Work your way up through your body. Depending on your knowledge of anatomy, you can be more or less specific.
3. If you find a spot that seems to be holding tension, mentally breath into that place and repeat '(arms/legs) go to sleep, (arms/legs) relax.'
4. You may well be asleep before you reach your head. You should find yourself gradually sinking into the bed, as if you're being pressed down by a gentle blanket.

CHAPTER SIX

Living in the present

Once you have taken the first steps down the road of meditation, you will find that you can apply the principles of a calm, detached mind to many aspects of your everyday life. And, subtly, your life will start to change.

As you become more tranquil, you will find that you seem to have more space to 'breathe' spiritually and emotionally. Working on your inner world will help you to feel centred and more certain of who you are. So you will become more confident. And because of this vigorous confidence, you will be more open to new experiences, and better able to cope with change.

Many people find that as they grow used to meditating regularly, they need to get in touch with their own spiritual natures. This takes people on very diverse journeys: from a Quaker meeting, to a sweat lodge, to the source of the Ganges – everyone's path is their own. The choice is yours. But if you do feel a pull to the numinous, follow your instincts and see where they take you. Areas of your life that have been stagnant may begin to move, while situations that have been unmanageably unstable may arrive at equilibrium.

Living with meditation

The most profound thing meditating can teach us is how to live in the moment. This means not thinking about the past – or the future – but focusing on the here and now.

Put like that it sounds simple, but spend a moment now and just watch the thoughts that stream through your mind. Do you find yourself recalling a comment from earlier in the day? Are you wondering about what you'll have for your next meal?

That's the past and future coming up to meet you. Just observe what kind of things you think about and categorise them into past, future and now.

Take a moment and try just thinking about now – your body, your hands. What can you see? Look at the colours, the textures. What can you smell? Every time your mind starts to speculate, bring it back to the present by focusing on your breathing. Then allow yourself to expand outwards again.

No one can spend a lifetime living completely in the moment – plans need to be made, people remembered. However, spending as much time as possible fully living each moment will have one simple effect: increased happiness. Living completely in the present rests your mind and, therefore, refreshes your spirit. How often have you spent a lovely day simply watching the world go by at the beach, or drinking in the gorgeous scenery when you go hiking? This kind of relaxation should not be confined to holidays and days off – every day of your life should have a little holiday in it. You should be able to get up in the morning and think, 'Wow, it's great to be alive.'

MINDFULNESS

The Buddhist notion of mindfulness is something that we can all use in our lives because it sets us free – at least temporarily – from our quotidian cares.

To be mindful simply means to pay attention (see also pp.92–3). But in this context it means more than that. Living mindfully means completely focusing on whatever task we have in hand – adding up figures, playing tennis, walking to school – whatever.

This has the effect of turning the task into a meditation. Try it with the next thing you do – even reading this sentence. Just focus in on this page and block out everything else: extraneous noise, smells, the sensations of your body. Immerse yourself in the act of reading – absorbing each word.

Maybe you did that for a moment. Now choose a task that's more routine; less full of surprises than this text. Making dinner is a good one. As you prepare the food go about each task with deliberation. You may realise that for certain tasks, especially creative ones, such as cooking, it's normal for you to enter a meditative state.

So now try really focusing when you're doing something you don't like – or something that bores you – like vacuuming, ironing or the accounts. Let the rest of the world fall away. Relax into your work.

Inner harmony

Theoretically, your chakra system should be continuously pulling in good energy and expelling bad energy. If this is functioning well, your ability to enjoy life will be enhanced.

The lower three chakras are connected to the practical side of life – making things manifest. The central ones are used when we relate to other people – through love and communication; and the top two are about our mental energy.

When the chakras are balanced all three of these aspects of our lives are working smoothly; but this is very unusual. Most people naturally have either more or less of one kind of energy. People with a lot of mental energy are often highly impractical; those who are good with money often lack a spark of imagination; people who spend a lot of time listening and counselling sometimes forget to get on with the cooking.

Which one are you?

This is a chakra balancing exercise (see panel, right) that requires quite a lot of time – and a certain amount of privacy because it involves sounds. Each chakra responds to a particular sound vibration. If you find this hard to believe, try it out, and you will be amazed.

CHAKRA BALANCING
Try doing this early in the morning before breakfast.

1. Sit comfortably and do your breathing until it's soft and natural. Make sure your body is quite relaxed. Relax your jaw.
2. Close your eyes and start to visualise your root chakra. Inhale, and as you exhale let the sound 'oh' escape from your lips. Don't push it out; let it slip out.
3. Do the same with each chakra, going up your body. Some sounds will come quite easily – you may falter over others. Do those again until the sound slips out easily. You should feel each sound resonating with that particular part of your body, like a violin bow.
4. Now go back down to the root chakra.
5. Do this as many times as you like. It can be kind of fun, like playing your whole body as a musical instrument.
6. Make sure you eat something after this meditation, and don't go out for an hour or two, as you may feel rather floaty.

CHAKRA SOUNDS

Crown Chakra – 'ng'

Third Eye Chakra – 'mm'

Throat Chakra – 'ee'

Heart Chakra – 'eh'

Solar Plexus Chakra – 'ah'

Sacral Chakra – 'oo'

Root Chakra – 'oh'

Coming and going

Nothing stays the same – even mountains erode, great rivers change direction and, of course, we grow older; our friends change, we encounter new people and create new situations.

Learning to live in the expectation of change is good. The Chinese call it 'tao', or flow. Every moment of every day we are part of this flowing of life energy. As new things come into our lives, the old are left behind. Our lives are in a constant state of becoming: an important part of this process is also dying.

Within our own bodies we are all in a continuous state of transformation and movement. Every now and then you might like to reflect on this and think about it as you breathe. With your inhalations you are breathing in new life, new energy; with your exhalations you are expelling old, used-up air.

You might even want to take this a step further. As you exhale think about how your dead energy gives something else new life – a plant can take the carbon dioxide that you breathe out and turn it into oxygen – your breathing is part of the great cycle of life on the planet. Your breath is part of the motion of being born and dying that takes place every moment.

Breathing into the cycle of life helps puts things in perspective. If you've had a busy day take a moment just to breathe. If you're feeling lonely – especially in a crowd – breathe in your connection with the web of life and then out.

There is no greater comfort in the darker moments of our lives than knowing that it will transform. Just breathe them out and breathe in new experience.

IN AND OUT

This is based on a Buddhist meditation that focuses on the cycle of life and death.

(01) Stand with your feet hip-width apart and your hands comfortably dangling at your sides. Make sure your back is straight and that you are relaxed. Your feet should be parallel. Bring your attention to your breathing for a while. When you are ready, focus on a spot, about the size of a large coin, in the centre of the crown of your head. It may begin to feel warm or tender.

(02) Think about energy coming and going out of that spot with your breath. You may visualise this energy as light. You can keep your meditation at this point, or you may want to continue.

(03) Allow the energy to flow down over your head and down your entire body in a wave. Then let it go back up again. Carry on feeling the coming and going. You may want to stop here, but you

can go further. Try to allow the energy waves to speed up, so they are flowing back and forth very fast, like electric currents. This is an advanced technique, so you may not achieve it when you first try. Stay with the coming and going for as long as you like.

01

02 03

Spirituality – meditation

Meditation is not a religion, but you can choose to use it as part of your own religious practice.

In the mystical traditions, enlightenment – even if it only lasts a split-second – means unity with the divine. All these traditions agree that 'God' is both inside you and outside you simultaneously. In psychoanalytic terms, one might say these beliefs lead to a dissolution of ego boundaries. Sometimes this is a useful thing – and sometimes it is not so handy – depending on your own inner stability and your current circumstances.

Eastern wisdom suggests that the material world – what we see, touch and feel – is an illusion and that reality is actually the world you contact in deep meditation; a world of spirit. If this idea appeals to you, you may want to explore it further.

Buddhists and Hindus both emphasise, for meditators, the importance of compassion or loving kindness. Even if you are a confirmed atheist you may want to include a blessing for all sentient beings at the end of your daily meditation. Simply think of sharing with the world the tranquillity you have experienced.

LOOKING AT 'GOD'

Meditating on a symbol, an idea or a religious mantra is a time-honoured technique for connecting with divine power. To start, you could try this method, which is adapted from one used by Buddhists.

1. Choose a religious image – an Old Master painting of Jesus on the Cross; an icon of the Virgin of Guadelupe; the word Jehovah in Hebrew script; or Allah in Arabic – the possibilities are endless.
2. Sit comfortably in your usual position with the image in front of you.
3. Look carefully at the image. Let it come in and out of focus. Try to keep your gaze still.
4. Now close your eyes and recreate the image in your mind's eye. Be as detailed as possible.
5. Open your eyes and gaze again.
6. Shut your eyes and recreate. You may want to do this several times. Eventually, keep your eyes shut and contemplate the inner image.

THE WORD
1. *Choose a piece of religious verse that appeals to you.*
2. *Now write your mantra deliberately, slowly, beautifully.*
3. *Write it over and over again; rhythmically and with focus. Pay attention to each word.*

The Prayer of Saint Francis
Lord, make me an instrument of thy peace.
Where there is hatred, let me sow love;
Where there is injury, pardon;
Where there is doubt, faith;
Where there is despair, hope;
Where there is darkness, light;
Where there is sadness, joy.
O divine Master, grant that I may not so much seek
To be consoled as to console,
To be understood as to understand,
To be loved as to love;
For it is in giving that we receive;
It is in pardoning that we are pardoned;
It is in dying to self that we are born to eternal life.

Let us attain life, let us attain strength. Let us attain action, let us attain dexterity in art, let us attain intellect and let us attain spiritual force. Let these celestial and terrestrial elements prolong our lives, protect our vitality, be our protectors and guard us.

ATHARVAVEDA

Index